Bruce Miller

I CAME, I SAW, I COFFEED

Online Dating: Why Doesn't He Call Me Back?

What Goes Through a Man's Mind on the First Meet?

Impressions from a Man who had Over 350 First Meetups.

By: Bruce Miller JD

Published by Team Golfwell.

I Came I Saw I Coffeed

Reviews:

"Insightful and fun to read. Enjoyed the stories and very true to life."

-J. Blake, Chicago

"Hard to put down. Each chapter was an adventure for Bruce and each woman was totally different from the others. A fun and entertaining read."

-T. Roberts, L.A.

"I liked the way each chapter was preceded by a relationship quote introducing the woman in the next chapter. Loved reading about how the relationships developed or didn't develop.

-B. Browning, NYC

"Hard to imagine Bruce met over 350 women. But, after reading about those in this book, I want to hear about the others. Keep these coming, Mr. Miller. Thank you.

C. Johnson, Chicago

Bruce Miller

Copyright © 2016 by Team Golfwell, all rights reserved. No part of this publication may be reproduced, distributed, or transmitted in any form or by any means, including photocopying, recording, or other electronic or mechanical methods, without the prior written permission of the publisher, except in the case of brief quotations embodied in critical reviews and certain other noncommercial uses permitted by copyright law.
Pacific Trust Holdings NZ Ltd.

Cover: King of Designer

ISBN: 9781991156556 Paperback

ISBN: 9781991156563 EPUB

Introduction

Have you ever wondered what goes through a man's mind when you first meet? "Why didn't he ask me out again? What did he think of me?" "Did I say the wrong thing?"

I was newly singled after an unwanted divorce and retired early, so I had time on my hands to find a girlfriend. I didn't want to be alone, and hadn't dated in years. I was eager to meet a woman, and became discouraged trying to find someone to be your love, your best trusted friend, a confidant and companion -- a very difficult task. Seeing my low spirits to get on with a search find a woman, a good friend simply told me dating is "Just a game of numbers -- the more ladies you meet, the better decision you'll make."

So, I ventured into the field of online dating and over three years met over 350 ladies. Many women asked me what goes through a man's mind when he meets a woman. In this book I spell out my thoughts about the women I met, her walk, her appearance, demeanor, clothes, habits, figure, etc. *in detail*.

I Came I Saw I Coffeed

How did I arrange on line to meet over 350 women? I simply explained I preferred meeting *in person* rather than trade potentially misunderstood messages on line. You can't hear voice inflections, or observe body language in a message. Most women agreed. Of course, some asked to first talk on the phone before meeting up which I did. Each evening, I searched the dating site, sending smiles or greetings to 20-30 women per day and got numerous replies the next day and proceeded to schedule them as best as I could.

Bruce Miller

All my life I enjoyed meeting new people. The women were fascinating, fun and interesting. Of course, I don't know what other men think and, obviously, the impressions I describe in this book are my own. I hope women who read this book will find it insightful, entertaining, amusing and useful. Names and places have been changed for privacy.

"It's not the impression you make -- it's the impression you leave. And, keep in mind you'll have to live up to that first impression, so it's best to be just yourself."

--Anonymous

Bruce Miller

Chapter 1.

Doctor Emma

Emma was a doctor whose husband divorced her to pursue another woman. Emma was now living alone in her very large home. We met for coffee where she worked.

I could tell by her nervous look when we sat down that she was brand new to online dating. I sensed she really didn't want to be there. I briefly told her about myself to put her at ease then asked her about her life. While she was giving me her history, I watched her nervously squirm in her chair. Her squirming unintentionally showed off her excellent figure. I kept smiling (while trying not to stare at her hips and legs) as she generalized about her life – I didn't hear it all as her curves kept distracting me as she contorted in her chair. Although she didn't realize it, she looked amazing to me. She could have told me she was a serial killer and I would just continue smiling at her.

Bruce Miller

After we finished, she got up to get back to work but seemed interested in me even though I was 10 years older, so I asked her to dinner the next evening and she kind of did a double take at my request, pause, then simply said "Okay."

The next evening, she walked out her front door as I was pulling up her long driveway. Dressed smart casually in an expensive way with just the right amount of jewelry, small earrings, a tennis bracelet, an expensive watch, and two tasteful rings, I thought she dressed to impress me but wasn't sure if she just hadn't dressed up in a while but she looked great. She wore a large brass buckled patent leather belt highlighting her slim waist. The restaurant wasn't far away and we were soon seated at a beautiful table by a window looking over a garden near the front of the restaurant (I assumed we got a nice table because the maître d' wanted to show her off to patrons). She smiled as we sat down, and I liked that.

She seemed reluctant to talk about herself; so being still amazed at her figure, I complimented her on her fitness.

Bruce Miller

"You must be a runner or a gym bunny, you're so fit!" I said.

"Yes, my ex-husband and I were runners," she said.

"The effects of your running show very well on you." I continued smiling trying to help her relax. "So did you regularly beat your husband?" She frowned. I rephrased: "I mean did you beat him *running?*"

"Oh, I'd like to beat him – in many ways. Haha! No, I didn't beat his times. What I really enjoy is swimming."

"Yes! I used to swim competitively in high school. Tell me about your swimming."

She lit up.

"On the weekday mornings we weren't running, we swam. We still do it. I love it and look forward to swimming almost more than working."

"But now that you're divorced, don't you feel awkward running and swimming with your ex-husband with everyone knowing he left you for another?"

Bruce Miller

She stared at me for a moment (she had amazing crystal blue eyes), then said, "He never lied to me. He came home one evening and told me he was leaving and going to live alone and had an interest in another woman. It was totally out of the blue -- I had no reason or warning he was going to do that."

"Did he move out right away?"

"He's a very bright man but he didn't have a clue where to live or how to set up a new home. So, I helped him find a place, selected furniture and helped him move."

What the hell? I didn't understand this. I'm not a psychologist but I can't believe she could be so calm telling me she helped him start a new life with another woman? So, I said, "What about, 'Hell hath not the fury...?'" She started to smile. I continued (not wanting to pry too much), "Why did he want to start a relationship with this woman?"

"She had worked with him for several years. He told me she'd continually compliment him on his techniques -- made him feel more appreciated than I did. But I had my own career."

"Yes, I know what you mean. Men like to be told we are the best at whatever we do, and I know that seems silly?"

She paused, then said, "I gave a talk to a medical convention overseas and he went along wanting to hear my talk but he left the auditorium towards the end of my speech. No compliments or appreciation – just ignored it. I didn't understand why he wasn't interested? I guess I just reciprocated indifference to him."

"Yeah, sounds like things starting rolling down hill, while he was getting lots of praise from a spectator?" I said. I looked at her face and saw her rage growing and about to erupt.

She was angry. "I just don't understand it! She's just average looking. Nothing special." Then she shouted, "What's wrong with me?!"

I looked over her shoulder and saw two gentlemen seated behind her smiling admirably at her and could easily tell they were thinking: *There's nothing wrong with you baby! Why don't <u>you</u> come over and sit with us?*

Bruce Miller

I started to chuckle. Here I was sitting with a very beautiful professional woman who could probably have any man in the place – yet her ex-husband left her feeling very insecure.

"Ah, how many dates have you been on since you divorced your husband?"

"You're the first."

I blinked in disbelief. "Oh, and how long has it been since he left?"

"Eighteen months."

I blinked again, then smiled. "And you go to bed by yourself every night? What a waste!"

She laughed. I looked around and saw the guys seated behind us had gotten back to their conversation.

I went on to date Emma but felt uncomfortable with the age difference between us. I was retired and she worked 50 to 60 hours a week. I was just getting use to retirement. Coming out of a bad marriage myself, I was reluctant to try and get serious and needed more time. I stayed in touch with Emma and still do to this day. She eventually paired up with another man closer to her age and a bit overweight who didn't even finish high school and grew up on the other side of the tracks. I figured he must have "other attributes" one of which was he made her feel very secure. Emma is happy with her new man and has been with him for several years now. Then I met an Uptown Girl in the next chapter.

"You asked me what would be the benefits of dating me? Ah.... You will be dating me. Do I need to repeat that to you?"

--Anonymous

Chapter 2

Vanessa

I first met Vanessa at an exclusive café in her posh suburb. She described herself as an "Uptown Girl" (like the one Billy Joel crooned about). Very attractive, and perhaps expensive to date, her profile was impressive.

I Came I Saw I Coffeed

Having thoughts she was out of my league, I waited at a table close to a front window reading my iPad and occasionally looking up for her. Twenty-five minutes had gone by and I was about to leave, when I saw Vanessa approaching.

It was worth the wait to see the way she paraded toward the cafe – head erect, shoulders back, confident and walking in the same tempo of upbeat music playing in the cafe. Her expensive outer coat and long blonde hair were flapping in the wind revealing a

Bruce Miller

designer dress and just the right amount of jewelry. She had steel blue eyes and looked much younger than the years she revealed on her profile.

I stood as she made her entrance into the café -- better described as a grand entrance. With a friendly smile on my face, I stood up to greet her. She responded with a poker face then kissed me on the cheek. She stared waiting for me to pull her chair out. I jumped to it.

A bit intimidated, I began the conversation. "You're quite an attractive lady and... say you look very much like my niece."

She eyed me up and down with the same poker face. "Do you have a picture of your niece?"

I was caught off guard but instantly realized I had my niece's picture on my iPad.

"Well.... as a matter of fact, I do." I swiped through the photos on my iPad and produced my niece's picture and showed it to her. Her eyebrows raised eyeing a younger likeness of herself standing next to my brother.

"Is this your brother?"

"Yes." I smiled, still wondering about her.

"He does resemble you. I'm not accustomed to dating sites and you're the second person I've ever agreed to meet for a coffee." She started to relax but still kept that poker face. She glanced again at the photo. "Yes, your niece does resemble me – but I looked different when I was her age, her cheekbones are higher than mine…." She again eyed me up and down. "You know you have to be careful who you meet."

"Yes, I understand. You're very unique, very attractive, very well to do…. I'm sure you get a lot of requests for meetups?"

"Not really."

"Why is that?" After I said that, I thought she might take that as my unintentionally questioning her veracity, but so what, I thought. It's probably more like a compliment to her good looks. She maintained the poker face.

"Men often look at me, but I'm really very shy."

I paused, then said, "It takes a bit of courage to get on a dating site to meet new people. I understand it's awkward."

"My girlfriend talked me into this. She filled out my profile. I'm not enjoying this."

We ordered coffees, then I resumed the conversation. "So you're divorced?"

"Yes, my husband left me for a younger woman. A foreign woman."

"Were you married a long time?"

"20 years. It was my first marriage and his second. My divorce took several years to finalize. My husband and I started a business (she told me the well-known business) with one store which we grew into many stores."

"Yes, I've seen your TV Commercials."

"We did it all together." Then, she went into detail about their business development and I wondered how she handled it all. Settling up a large business is a complicated and a long drawn out divorce on top of that is very tough.

"Have you had any relationships after the divorce?" I asked.

"Yes. Tom helped me through the divorce. He was a friend of both of ours, a builder, very intelligent. When my husband left, we lived together for a while."

"What happened to Tom,"

"Tom's not coming back."

The response dumbfounded me. He lived with her and helped her through a very rough time - they obviously loved each other? So I asked, "Why isn't he coming back?"

"I threw a tray at him."

"Oh... did you hit him?"

"No."

Still wondering, I asked, "Why did you throw the tray at him?"

"He was late." She replied with that poker face looking for my reaction.

I bit both of my cheeks trying not to laugh. This was an honest and sincere lady. I paused and smiled. "Well, life has its ups and downs – "

She interrupted, "We're still friends but I'm looking for a full time partner."

"Oh, I see, you had me going – "

"I did throw the tray at him." She interrupted and we both laughed.

I was intrigued. "Would you like to go out to dinner with me?" I don't know why I asked her right away. I didn't even explain my own background. I somehow felt it was the right moment to ask as I felt a good connection growing between us. She stared at me hearing my request for another date, then smiled.

"Sure."

I pulled into a long driveway to her three story home with pool, tennis court, etc., etc. She lived alone with a very large German Shepard named "Max". They both greeted me at the door. She told me she was still getting ready and handed me a tennis racquet and ball and told me to go into the court and hit tennis balls to Max while she finished getting ready.

"He hasn't had his exercise today."

As soon as she handed me the tennis racket and ball, Max was doing his "Happy ball dance" and led me to the court and I began hitting a few lobs to Max. He retrieved all of them and ran back dropping the ball at my feet. After a while, I heard a "Here Max!" Max ran to Vanessa.

We left for the restaurant, had dinner, learned more about each other, and returned to her home.

As we drove up, she asked me in for a coffee and I agreed. I sat in the lounge on a leather couch and Max jumped on the couch next to me and stared at me. Vanessa joined us carrying the infamous tray and two Irish coffees and sat down next to me. Max was still staring.

We finished the coffee and I gently put my arm around Vanessa and kissed her keeping an eye open on Max.

"Don't mind him, he knows if I don't like something. He likes you."

"Ah, yes, I guess?" I continued to kiss her and we kissed for about 10 minutes and it started to get passionate. I heard a soft whine. If I didn't stop myself, I wondered if Max would stop me. But I didn't care. The passion continued. As I penetrated her, Max jumped off the couch and I thought for an instant I would lose my erection, but Max just stood next to me. I was caught up in the passion and continued thrusting and she was moaning in a nice way which kept Max calm.

    I continued seeing Vanessa for a year and Max became my buddy. It took time, but I learned Vanessa was her own person. She did whatever she wanted and usually got whatever she wanted – she had more balls than most men. She expected me to pay for all our outings as "That is what men do," according to her. I admired her yet sometimes felt like an accessory. She eventually asked me to move in but specified a rent way above one-half of the ongoing costs which made me feel more like a customer than a partner. So, I declined and remained in my own home and continued to date her. She was quite attractive and wouldn't flirt with any other man (I liked that very much).

Bruce Miller

She was a "head turner" and when she walked into a room to meet me, it made me feel special.

She is a lady I admire very much, but I was looking for a soul mate. I tried to make her aware I wanted a soul mate -- a partner. But she wasn't interested in another partner – at least not yet. And she really didn't need one anyway.

Vanessa and I are still very good friends today and she's dating Tom again but still lives alone with Max by her side.

"First impressions are important.

While you shouldn't judge a book by

its cover, you probably won't read it

if the cover is not inviting."

-Anonymous

Chapter 4

Susan

Arriving ten minutes early to meet Susan, I sat there checking my phone for emails when I felt a light tap on my shoulder. I turned and saw Susan standing behind me. She looked just like her picture. I stood up. "Hi Susan! Yes, please sit down." My eyes immediately shot to her large shapely breasts and deep cleavage and felt a stirring in my groin. I blinked my eyes from her chest to her smiling blue eyes. I was impressed with the breasts. I thought about past times seeing amazing pictures of women on line only to be disappointed when meeting them in person. This was not one of them.

"Let me get you a coffee?" I said. After ordering at the counter, I returned and said, "Thank you for coming, Susan. Tell me about yourself?"

"Oh, I want to hear about you first."

Bruce Miller

I explained my background briefly then paused, "Susan, my life's boring. Tell me about *you*." She blinked her eyes, seeming a bit surprised I didn't continue talking.

"I'm surprised you don't talk more about yourself. Most men talk for 45 minutes about themselves, how much money they have, their ex-wives, jobs, blah, blah. You're the first one who wants to learn about me! Now I'm getting scared. Haha!"

"You're a great looking woman and men want to impress you."

"Well, I've been on this dating site for about 2 years and I'm still looking. Most of these just end with a coffee for me."

"That's hard to believe...just one coffee?"

She smiled. "Well, I was married for 20 years when my husband divorced me for a younger model. Took me by surprise. He was having an affair. I'd been faithful to him and worked hard for him in his business. After the divorce, I let my hair down and met a lot of men and told myself it was time to party." She bounced in her chair as she talked. I kept focused on her eyes.

"So you partied?"

"Yes. I had relationships with two very nice men, but both broke up. So I got on the dating site – there's really no other way to meet anyone." We talked on. There wasn't anything unusual about her and we were getting on well. So, I asked her out for dinner.

At dinner, we continued talking over drinks. She hadn't eaten and the alcohol quickly got to her through an empty stomach. She began swaying back and forth, but she was having a great time.

"What went wrong with your last boyfriend?" As I said that, I noticed her hair had oddly shifted. She read my face and raised her eyes.

"Yeah, I wear a wig." She shifted the wig back in place.

"Gosh I couldn't tell. Why?" I asked.

"A while ago, I was diagnosed with cancer. I went through chemo and came out of it a few months ago. The cancer is gone and, like everyone says, the chemo was worse than the cancer. "My hair is growing back and I'm feeling better now, but there's something else I should tell you before we go any further."

"What's that?" I asked.

"As I said, my husband divorced me for a younger model and I partied a lot. Well, I've got mild genital herpes. It doesn't bother me very much but makes it difficult to find a partner."

That stopped me cold, but I was puzzled. "The herpes didn't stop you from having two relationships that went on for a few years?" I asked.

"The condition didn't bother them." I glanced at her attractive figure and understood. She was honest and sincere. Everyone admires that but I couldn't help overthinking herpes. The conversation dwindled and she left shortly thereafter.

I knew she was a quality woman and felt very sorry for her. There were others to meet, and I met another with more serious problems in the next chapter.

Bruce Miller

"I was always attracted not by some quantifiable, external beauty, but by something deep down, something absolute. Just as some people have a secret love for rainstorms, earthquakes, or blackouts, I liked that certain undefinable something directed my way by members of the opposite sex. For want of a better word, call it

magnetism. Like it or not, it's a kind of power that snares people and reels them in."

--Haruki Murakami, South of the Border, West of the Sun

Chapter 5

Theresa

Theresa, a school teacher, had been online dating for a few years but lost interest and let her premium membership expire. I found her about 15 pages deep in an age range search. Her picture stopped me cold. I wasn't sure why her picture impressed me so much. Someone told me the picture of the person who is right for you automatically generates a good feeling. This is because, chemicals are involuntarily released in your brain when you see the right person for you giving you a very pleasant feeling.

Well, a very pleasant feeling came over me when I stopped at Theresa's picture. With average looks, she sat in a large stuffed chair with a slight smile wearing white shorts. Her bare feet were resting on the front edge of the seat with her knees were open and her forearms were propped up on her knees. Her legs were attractive. I messaged her an invite for a coffee and she responded about a week later.

    I sat in the café ten minutes early looking at the front door when my peripheral vision caught a figure approaching from the side. Before I turned, I was tapped on the shoulder and heard a natural and relaxed voice say, "Hey you."

    "Ha! You must be Theresa." I said.

    "The same," she happily replied.

    "Wow, I didn't recognize you at first. You look much better than your picture." I said.

She had gotten to the cafe early and waited in the back of the café to check me out. I admired her cautiousness. Most of the others were 5 minutes late. I asked why she took a week to respond to my invite for a coffee.

"I don't check my messages. I've been on the site a while and losing interest."

"So tell me about yourself?" I asked.

"You first." She said. So, I gave her my history. As I talked, she listened intently -- her eyes growing large at interesting parts and narrowing at bad parts. Hey, I thought, she's

actually paying attention. "So, your profile says

you were a teacher?"

"I taught first grade."

"So, you're nice looking and you seem

very smart. I imagine a lot of guys want you."

She smiled but didn't respond.

"Oh, I get it. You're a heartbreaker aren't

you? When was your last relationship?" She

drew back in her chair with a blank look on her

face. Not being sure of what was wrong, I

didn't pursue an answer. I changed the subject.

"Hey, tell me about your family."

We talked on. We were getting along so I said, "By the way, how am I doing with you?" I wouldn't have asked that question if our conversation wasn't going well.

"You're doing ok," she smiled back. So, I asked her to dinner and we agreed to meet at the restaurant a few days later.

She began to open up more at the restaurant and was telling me about her life, her plans for the future, her toddler grandchild, her son, church and Naturism.

Naturism? I raised an eyebrow. *A church going nudist?* "Oh, you like nudism?" I said.

"Yes I do. I go to a nudist beach but just go topless keeping my bottoms on."

I glanced at her chest. She was small breasted but I hadn't ever been to a nude beach. She read my face.

"Oh, it's totally appropriate. There's no sex taking place. Just naturalists."

"Yeah, sounds interesting. Say, you know I'm an agnostic and not a big church goer. Are you a regular Church goer?"

"I use to go regularly when my son was growing up, then didn't go for years. When I got sick I began going every day."

"What happened?"

"I had cancer and went through surgery and the Doctor got it all but told me there's no guaranty the cancer won't come back."

Bruce Miller

"I understand, there's no atheists in fox holes."

We talked briefly about her recovery. Then I asked, "So, tell me about your relationships?" She looked away. I was interested in her, so I waited for her to answer. After a long pause, she said, I had relationships over the years but nothing seemed to last more than two or three years. After my son grew up, I met a John, a commercial pilot. We lived together in my home."

"Sounds like you finally found someone. What happened?"

"He was away when I was told I had cancer. It had a major effect on him as well and we started to grow apart and he'd be away more and more. After I recovered from the operation, I had to go away for six months to help my mother. When I got back, I found another woman moved into my home with her children."

"Eh, what?" I blinked.

Bruce Miller

"I arrived back and was walking through my house and saw toys in a bedroom and the cleaning lady stopped me and told me another woman moved into the house while I was away."

"That's insane!"

"While I was away helping my mother, John told me he would buy the house from me. We knew we were separating and I wanted to sell my house and he was going to buy it. But when he moved a young woman in with her two children, without asking me, I called everything off and they all left."

If you looked up dumbfounded in the dictionary you would see a picture of my face at this point. I wasn't sure what to say, but it was difficult for me to imagine the pain she had gone through. I felt very sorry for her but we ended the dinner with casual conversation.

I didn't ask her out but called her the next day to see how she was doing and she had her 3-year-old grandson over and was having lots of fun and laughter with him. We dated a few

Bruce Miller

times and I was interested in her but my spark

for her dwindled. She'd been through a lot and

I wasn't much for Church or Naturism. Today,

we're still friends and stay in touch.

"Sometimes, you can't explain what you see in a person. It's just the way they take you to a place where no one else can. In the same manner, you can't force chemistry where none exists; and you can't deny it when chemistry is there. And, if you try very hard to push for chemistry, it's like a fart, if you push really hard, all you may get is shit."

-Anonymous

Chapter 6

Rebecca

Rebecca's face on the dating site jumped out at me. She looked young for her years with a sparkling, well dressed and relaxed look that captured me. There was something about her smile – to me, it somehow revealed she was very happy with herself.

We met at a café and she walked in wearing that happy smile with a graceful and energetic, and upright and purposeful walk. She looked focused and although most would say she just had average looks, or, she was just another face in the crowd, I was attracted to her but didn't know why. She didn't look like anyone I'd ever known in the past. Thinking back, I guess it was her demeanor and the way she carried herself which made her so attractive.

When Rebecca sat down we told each other our background. She was a lawyer with a small firm and previously married to an accountant – 10 years her junior (I was a few years older than her and had a fleeting thought a younger man might be a tough act to follow). She told me a story I heard many times. Out of the blue her husband told her he'd fallen in love with another woman. It devastated her. So much so, she joined a worldwide group of newly separated/divorced women trying to cope and readjust to single life. I admired her for taking action instead of feeling sorry for herself.

    She saw my admiration. "When I speak to our group, I'm actually really helping myself to readjust. Listening to other women's problems takes my mind off myself and helps me readjust."

I asked her how many online dates she had with people from the dating site. "Not very many," she said. "I'm busy with my practice and I'm not even sure I have time for someone in my life, but I do want to eventually meet someone."

During our conversation, I couldn't tell if she had any interest in me. The conversation seemed matter of fact. I looked for something, a voice inflection, a sparkle in her eye, or body language telling me she was interested in seeing me again. I was losing enthusiasm and our coffee conversation dwindled. But, I was interested in her so I just simply asked if she wanted to have a dinner date and she gave me a nonchalant "Yes I would."

    After I heard her neutral reply, I wished I hadn't asked for another date, but wanted to get to know her. I assumed she simply agreed to a second date to learn more about me but knew I hadn't given her a spark. Then again, I really had no clue how she felt.

I Came I Saw I Coffeed

Driving home, I had more negative thoughts so I called her and left a message on her voice mail, telling her I didn't realize but had something else to do and would call and reschedule the date later. Two weeks went by and as I met other women from the dating site, I still kept thinking about her. So, I called her and she answered saying, "I'm surprised you called. I thought you weren't going to call me."

"Rebecca, I would like to get to know you very much, but I just thought you didn't take any interest in me so I took my time calling you."

"What made you think that," she asked?

"Well, you seemed indifferent when I asked you on a second date and I didn't want to waste your time."

"Oh, very sorry, I didn't mean to give you that impression. Remember, I've got a busy practice but I *certainly* would like to meet you again. A couple I know is going to the theatre this Saturday night and asked me to join them.

Would you like to go? I'll arrange for the tickets."

Wow! I thought. There wasn't any spark in our first meeting but this was more than I expected. I was glad she suggested an event with another couple. That made it easy for me to accept since it would be more relaxed and perhaps no dangling conversations this time? I wasn't sure what would happen, but thought I'd give it a try.

We went and had a nice time – well, as good as could be expected. But, there wasn't any chemistry. We continued to date a couple more times, then we mutually decided to be "friends" and keep in touch.

    Taken aback by her indifference toward me, I wondered if anyone would take an interest in me. My late grandmother told me when I first started dating, *"Some women you like won't like you. And there will be women you don't like who will like you. So let nature take its course. Don't be in a rush."*

"Men truly want brighter, more articulate, aggressive women. They want to be seen in the world with them. But they also want these women to leave some of it at the doorstep. These guys love their wives. They just haven't figured out what to do when that strength is channeled toward them."

--Terrence Real quotes

Chapter 7

Barbara

As a general rule, I don't give out too much information on my online profile as the reader may draw the wrong conclusions since words can be misunderstood. Again, it's a lot easier to learn what a person is like by meeting them in person so you experience them and see her facial expressions, etc.

I Came I Saw I Coffeed

    A coffee or glass of wine meetup doesn't take much time. If a woman replied to my initial, "I would like to meet you" message, I was surprised about 90% agreed. There isn't anything special about me. I'm an average retired business man, not rich or flashy. Most ladies told me my profile is "average", and I'm average looking. And, going back to my grandmother, I met a woman who needed someone very much and took a liking to me, but I wasn't sure I liked her. It went like this:

Bruce Miller

 I got a message from a very nice looking woman, brunette with beautiful well-kept hair and blue eyes. She asked to meet for a coffee or a wine. I liked her head shot picture and she was 5 foot 6 inches which seemed right for my 6-foot height, so I agreed. She was a nurse and recently out of a relationship (I sympathize with women who are just out of relationships as most want to just talk to a man to help get them back on track). Very few initially contact me. I understand women think it's forward and assume men take a dim view of women initiating contact, but it really doesn't matter to me. I enjoy meeting women who want to get back on track and not feel sorry for themselves.

I saw from her profile she lived in my neighborhood, so we met at a nearby cafe. When she arrived we talked some then I asked her how long she'd lived in the neighborhood.

"Just moved in a few weeks ago. Where do you live?" I told her and thought if it didn't work out between us, at least I might have another friend in the neighborhood. She worked at a hospital about 2 miles away as a triage nurse in the ER. She was above average

Bruce Miller

looking with a thin face, but her pictures or profile didn't reveal she was around 180 lbs.

She was just out of a two-year relationship. I asked her what happened.

"We lived together in his apartment near the coast for a year and a half. He has a large fishing boat and we'd go out fishing and I loved it. He was almost retired and life was ideal for us."

"So why did you break up?" I asked.

"Another woman turned his eye." I gave her a sympathetic look.

She vented. "He told me he had another woman and I had to move out, but *I wasn't going that easy!* I took my time, thinking he'd get tired or bored with an attractive woman 13 years younger than him."

I nodded showing I understood. "Barbara, I know what you're talking about. Have you ever heard that old saying, 'Show me the most beautiful woman in the world and I'll show you a man who's grown tired of having sex with her.' There's got to be more than just sex or beauty."

"Yeah, he even brought her home while I was there."

"Whaaat? Why'd he'd do that?"

"He was trying to get me out quick. He brought her in thinking I'd leave. But, I wasn't going to leave while she was there! I'm not afraid to stand up for myself. I was gradually moving out and he just... brought her in! She paraded herself around the apartment in front of me showing she was the boss now."

"Wow! Did you start throwing...eh, marshmallows at her?"

"I wanted to do worse -- to both of them! But I kept cool -- 'Cooler heads prevail.'"

I nodded agreement and admired her anger management.

"What did he do while she paraded around?"

"He was totally indifferent! God! I'm glad I'm rid of the heartless man! Someday he'll realize what a mistake he made."

Bruce Miller

I paused a bit, feeling sorry for her and what she'd went through then asked, "How long ago did this happen?"

"Two months ago. I moved out, lived with a girlfriend, then bought this home." She was still hurting very much and still loved the guy. Tears came to her eyes, then she asked me if I would go on a fishing charter with her. I could see she was very vulnerable and wanted company but I had to think about this since she lived so close to me, so I didn't answer right away. She felt the pause, then asked me to come over for dinner.

I Came I Saw I Coffeed

I started to shake my head, then said, "I'm not sure. You seem to still love him very much and you're vulnerable and I'm not sure I want to get involved. You seem to need more time to get back to your old self?"

"No. I need a friend. There's not many men around."

"I ah...."

"It's hard to meet single men. How old are you?"

Bruce Miller

I paused and smiled. "I'm about the same age as you. How old was your indifferent fish boat guy?"

"Three years younger than me. Oh, and we loved sex. I enjoy sex. I'll bet you could use a cuddle?" She leaned toward me.

I looked at my watch and felt sorry for her. I'm no psychologist but not many women will initiate talk about sex and I she was being herself, but I didn't want to flatly reject her. So, I told a white lie, "Well, there's another woman I recently met and… I'm not sure if it's going to work, but I want to see where it will go. Right now, I ah... got to get going. It was nice meeting you and I'm sure we'll see each other from time to time."

As I left, she asked me for my phone number. I gave it to her feeling sorry for her. She tried to call me then next day and left a message she'd like to go on a fishing charter. I didn't return the call, then saw her coming up my stairs through my front window about an hour after the telephone call. She knocked on my door. I wanted to but didn't answer.

Bruce Miller

Fortunately, I had another friend who recently learned he had a medical condition and thought he might be interested in meeting her. He was a very wealthy single guy and a gentleman. But I'm not a matchmaker. I called her back and told her I didn't want to go fishing with her since it might hurt my chances with the woman I was interested in. She understood.

Crazy as this sounds, a few days later, my friend, the wealthy guy, knew I was on line meeting women and asked me if I knew anyone interesting he could meet. I told him I knew several women and gave him a general

I Came I Saw I Coffeed

description of some ladies. I described Barbara to him and he took her number. About three weeks later, we ran into each other and he thanked me as he and Barbara were dating. His spirits were up, he bought a fabulous new car, and I wished him and Barbara the best.

Bruce Miller

"If a woman has a job, has her own car, pays her bills, and manages to live comfortably before she meets you, a man understands she wants loyalty and not his money since she can finance herself. And being a single woman doesn't mean nobody wants you. It means you're pretty, sexy and you're taking your time deciding how you want your life to be and who you want to spend it with."

--Your Tango

Chapter 8

Carol

When I first went on the dating site, I received a message from Carol, a blue eyed brunette, saying she read my profile and wanted to meet me. I saw from her profile; she'd been on the site for 3 years. She left her phone number in the message, so I called her and asked where we should meet as I lived 40 miles away from her.

"Oh, I'll drive out to you," she said.

Surprised, I simply answered, "Yeah, that's fine, but how about a place half way between us?"

"No, no, I like to drive and know your suburb well."

We met the next day at a nearby café. "So, you've been on the site for 3 years? I'm surprised you haven't paired up with someone?"

"Oh, I've dated a few guys for several months, but I guess... I must be too picky."

"Why did you contact me?"

"You were new to the dating site. When you first go on the site, you're featured as a 'New Member' and you get a lot of attention when you first go on. I make it a point to greet new men right away or some other woman will snatch him."

"Haha! Great! Snatch me up, please,"

"Okay, take me to dinner."

Bruce Miller

"You like burgers?"

"Sure."

I wasn't sure what I was getting myself into but she seemed bright, happy and assertive. I took her to a quiet place which featured amazing burgers. We discussed our lives and future aspirations but not a spark was there. I asked her out one more time, but still no spark. We went our separate ways.

About two weeks later, I was sitting in a café talking to a new woman when Carol walked by with a girlfriend. Carol stopped and waved at me but didn't approach. I smiled and waved back.

The next day, Carol called me and said, "That woman you were with is not right for you." I wondered why she would bother to call me but kept silent to see where this was going to go. She continued, "She's not good looking. You look odd as a couple."

"Thanks for your concern Carol. How are you doing?"

"Did you see my girlfriend? She was walking with me when we passed you. The redhead?"

"No, I didn't notice her."

"She wants to meet you. She's much better for you. She's 5' 8" with great figure and she's interested!"

Why the hell is she sticking her nose in my business? I thought more for a moment realizing I'm single and don't have anyone I'm interested in, so I told her, "Okay, I'll call her."

I Came I Saw I Coffeed

I called Carol's friend and met her the next day and she was gorgeous. A model doing Television Commercials (TVCs as she referred to them), she was nice but our minds were on different planes. Although she was a trophy to have on your arm and lots of romance in the evenings, there wasn't much else. I would ask her about her goals in life and she would respond that she had a dog and then tell me about the dog. I asked her where she got the dog and why she picked that dog, and she'd say, "I liked him." Conversation was difficult and I was boring to her.

Bruce Miller

I'm still friends with Carol and she's still

looking and I think someday, she'll find the man

of her dreams (whether he wants Carol or not)

since Carol doesn't seem to take no for an

answer. She isn't afraid to reach out for what

she wants.

"We are all a little weird, and life's a little weird. And when we find someone whose weirdness is compatible with ours, we join up with them and fall in mutual weirdness and call it love."

-Dr. Seuss

Chapter 9

Janice

I read Janice's profile with great interest since she commented how difficult it was to meet the right person. Feeling the same, I understood how she felt.

After briefly messaging back and forth, we exchanged telephone numbers and talked over the phone several times. She explained she preferred to talk to see if I "pass the test" as someone she would like to get to know. I didn't think much of her request since I understood she didn't want to waste our time.

We talked for about an hour on the phone. There was a lot of miles between us, so she invited me to meet her in her home and I was welcome to stay overnight and drive back the next morning. Fantastic!

I did the two-and-a-half-hour drive then, took her to lunch and we along. Then we walked the beach for a few hours getting to know each other. She was looking for a permanent partner. I was looking for the same. She was an intelligent woman. But at times she talked too much (I enjoy hearing a woman talk and try to listen with an understanding mind but she was over the top). For example, she would start talking about her sister who lived in Canada and continue talking for twenty minutes straight bringing in a trip she took to Machu Picchu, her car problems, dishonest mechanics, the Canadian Government, her health and operations, nude swimming, beach sex, her cat, etc.

"Am I talking too much?" She'd ask me in the middle of a sentence.

"No, I'm listening."

My head was spinning. I only knew she was finished talking when I didn't hear any more words. I had read about listening. Most men in this crazy competitive world are trained to listen like lawyers preparing their counter arguments as the other person speaks. He's thinking how he will reply. But if I'm hearing a long narrative, I get bored.

Women seem to talk at length for to hear someone understand what they feel. They seem not to want a reply – only some indication the listener understands her feelings.

Janice had a beautiful voice and her inflections and humor made her easy to listen to, but, she kept changing subjects without waiting for a reply. We sat down on the sand on wide vacant beach with no one else on the beach for as far as you could see. All of a sudden, she got extremely nervous and kept turning to look at the high mounds of beachgrass about 150 yards behind us.

"What's wrong?" I asked.

"Oh nothing."

"You seem a bit agitated? You okay?"

She continued looking at the bluff behind us. I stared at her until she finally blurted out, "I think I just saw my ex-husband."

"Where?" There was still no one else on the beach."

"I think he's watching us from the mound behind us."

"Did you see him?" I asked.

"I think so."

I got up and walked back to the mound and looked around.

"There's no one here." I assured her.

"Oh. Okay. Must be all in my head. He's spied on me in the past."

Wow! I thought. The move from Canada must have been stressful. I didn't know if her talkative nature was a result of her former husband or if she was just that way. Starting a new relationship with someone is difficult and problems usually arise. We all have issues and we all know that. So, I think it's best to peel the onion slowly. It's easier to understand another's problems if you've been with them a while and not the first date.

When I left the next morning, I thanked her promising to catch up but knew she wasn't right for me. And neither was the next one.

Bruce Miller

"They can beg and they can plead,

But they can't see the light, that's right

'Cause the boy with the cold hard cash

Is always Mr. Right. 'Cause we are

Living in a Material World

And I am a material girl...."

--Madonna

Chapter 10

Diane

Diane was an executive assistant to the CEO of a large company. She had been divorced a year. We agreed to meet for a glass of wine in the late afternoon after she got off work. Her ex-husband was a tradesman and earned a fairly good living. They had a nice home in the

Bruce Miller

suburbs. I got to the hotel lounge about 10 minutes early.

      She spied me right away as she marched enthusiastically into the lounge of a downtown hotel exactly on time with a big smile on her face. Wow! She had an impressive walk and manner about herself. She exuded confidence. As we talked, I learned her job exposed her to the finer things in life (i.e. private jets, making reservations in grand hotels, exotic locations, etc.). She gradually became unsatisfied with an average life and divorced her husband.

I knew I couldn't give her those things but I was curious to meet her. "I'm not trying to be an armchair quarterback or any kind of critic, and I understand you did what you chose to do, but seems to me you had it all? A husband who earned a good living and who loved you very much and a nice home?"

Her eyes looked away. I paused and continued. "Well...why did you venture out from your marriage."

Bruce Miller

"Hindsight is always 20/20 and yes, I had a good life but I want more. We've only got one life and I wasn't getting younger." She said.

"I'm not questioning your judgment, but do you think you took your husband for granted?"

"Not really." She shot back.

"If -- and I'm just saying, 'if' -- things don't work out for you, are you going back to your husband?"

"No, he's met another woman."

I paused. She's here to see if I fit her shopping list. I continued. "So have you been meeting the right people? Found anyone who fits your criteria?"

"I wouldn't be sitting here if I did. Your profile interested me and I want to meet you." She ended that sentence with a very warm smile. "After I went through the divorce, I dated executives, professional people, even a politician. And, I'm very careful not to get into the same situation I was in before."

"What do you mean?"

Bruce Miller

"I'm in my 40s and there are a lot of exciting people in the world. Most women don't have any idea about the real exciting things in life. I have a strong desire to live and I'm expensive. How are you financially?"

I felt I was now in a job interview rather than meeting someone to love. I wasn't ready to discuss my financials with her. If she were an accountant, or investment advisor, I might have given her some general information. Her attitude came across clearly. If you want to go further with me, you better have the qualifications.

I Came I Saw I Coffeed

I was getting annoyed. Then again, it was refreshing to see a woman get to the point without wasting time. I began to admire her. But as soon as I had a slight feeling of admiration, negative thoughts of meeting a material girl raced through my mind. She sat across from me as calm as she could be smiling at me waiting for my financial status. Her calmness made me realize why women generally live longer than men. She saw me thinking, then began to look for her purse.

"I'm okay financially but not sure I want to discuss details. That's important to you isn't it?"

She picked up her purse with one hand and finished her wine with the other and began to say goodbye – I stopped her with a motion of my hand to wait. I looked her in her eye. "I admire your candor about what you want in life and I think you're going to get what you want. I understand."

She smiled. I added a further thought, and was chuckling at her attitude. "Oh, for what it's worth, if I want something, I first picture myself having it to see if I really enjoy it? In other words, *wanting* something is a lot different than *having*, if you know what I mean?"

"Oh, I will get what I want. I usually do and I will enjoy my life." She smiled and left and to this day I still wonder if she did get what she wanted. I suspect she did. Then I went from "Ms. I Want It All" to "Ms. Fun."

Bruce Miller

"This is all you need to know.

Women are crazy and men are stupid.

The main reason women are crazy is

because men are stupid.

-George Carlin

Chapter 11

Brenda

Brenda, a PhD in physics, worked in medical research. A brilliant woman who went back to school to get her Doctorate after leaving a career as a physio therapist. She never married, had no children, and a wealthy

Bruce Miller

boyfriend for 10 years and travelled a lot with him until he left her for a younger model.

    We arranged to meet after she got off work in the hotel lounge – the same hotel lounge where I had met Diane in the previous chapter. Brenda walked in smiling ear to ear. Her expensive top revealed most of her breasts which jiggled boldly announcing her presence (in stereo with double speakers) as she walked through the lobby toward me. Men's heads turned to watch her "DIY" floor show.

After we exchanged the usual greetings, we sat down at a remote table and I ordered two glasses of wine.

"Do you like my tits?" She asked happily. Her demeanor showed she was a happy lady with a permanent smile on her face.

"Haha! Yes, I like what I see!"

"I just got them a few months ago." She bounced in her chair then continued. "I was very flat chested and I didn't want to get *really* big ones."

Bruce Miller

"They're very attractive…. Say, let's raise our glasses!" I said.

"What are we toasting to?"

"To your tits!"

We laughed hard. I asked her out right then and there and we dated for a while.

She was a lover of life and took wonder at a lot of things I took for granted. "Look at the skyline!" "What a marvelous day." "I have so much energy." "Can you do the Dougie?" She got up and danced the Dougie, showing me how to do the dance while chanting, "...All the bitches love it..."

This lady was fun. This was a keeper -- if she took a liking to me, but I can't dance and she laughed at my attempts.

We dated for a while. But her research position came to a close and she moved far away for a teaching position at a university. We stay in touch from time to time but distance is a problem, of course.

Bruce Miller

I was about to walk out the door when I

met the next one.

"When you see a person, do you just concentrate on their looks? It's just a first impression. Then there's someone who doesn't catch your eye immediately, but you talk to them and they become the most beautiful thing in the world. The greatest actors aren't what you would call beautiful sex symbols."

-- Brad Pitt

Chapter 12

Linda

I walked into the café ten minutes early and sat down waiting for Linda to appear. After twenty minutes, I heard a soft voice behind me, "Are you....?"

"Yes, I am! And you must be Linda?" I stood up, turned and greeted her with a warm smile which slowly dissolved on my face as I scanned her head to toe – hair akimbo beaten with an eggbeater (a definite bad hair day), tattered top with a plunging neckline, crinkly tight pants, old faded orange flip flops on her feet, black toe polish -- but a smiling face with large blue sparkling eyes eager to meet me.

Immediately, I felt sorry for her and curious to hear her story. Her profile picture was quite attractive. But, in person, she was (I guess you would politely say) "different"?

Bruce Miller

"So how long have you been on the dating site," I asked.

"About 2 years. It's hard to meet the right man."

I bit my cheek. "Yeah, hard to meet the right woman too. Tell me about it," I said. "Say your picture --"

"Yes, haven't got around to changing it yet. Do you think I can still get away with it?"

I paused and thought of a quote often heard about online dates, *"If you don't look like your picture, you're buying me drinks 'till you do."* Then decided not to say that and instead said, "You've got a nice look, Linda, would you like a coffee?"

I thought if this woman made the effort to meet me, I'll respect that even though I wanted to leave. I ordered coffees at the counter and returned forcing a smile as I sat down. "So, tell me about yourself?" I listened to her life story as she talked on and on. I began to drift off wondering if she purposely had perfect messy hair? No, I thought it was more like an "Accept me as I am" look. Very bold, I thought, and she continued to talk on. She saw I drifted off and raised her voice.

"There's something *very special* about me," she half shouted. I looked up and her bright blue eyes capturing my attention again.

"Oh? Tell me," I quietly said hinting she lower her voice.

"I'm psychic!"

"You're psycho?" I mumbled.

"No, I'm a psychic. Been that way ever since I can remember."

"Yes, I'm a bit familiar with the sixth sense. Tell me more."

She now gave me the psychic history of her life filled with amazing intuition experiences. I had heard psychics before so I wondered if she was ever practical with it and interrupted, "Why don't I take you to a horse track and you can pick a few winners?"

"Doesn't work like that. Things just come to me. I can't force it," she said.

"So, ...we've never met before.... What do you see about us?"

Linda paused with a serious look on her face. "You already have someone -- no wait – there are several women in your life but you're not sure about any of them."

Yeah, I thought, very true about single people. Linda read my face and continued, "We're going to be good friends." We continued talking and she was right, we're still good friends after 3 years. She checks up on me (like a mom) from time to time and asks how

I'm doing. She found a very nice man and peculiarly, they look very similar and if I didn't know better, I'd mistake them for a brother and sister. His hair was a bed head too. She's very happy with him. I don't know if she foresaw him psychically in her life. She says she didn't –

"It just happened."

Bruce Miller

"All I'm telling you to do is to be smart about it. Know that if this man isn't looking for a serious relationship, you're not going to change his mind just because you two are going on dates and being intimate. You could be the most perfect woman on the Lord's green earth-you're capable of interesting conversation, you cook a mean breakfast, you hand out backrubs like sandwiches, you're independent (which means, to him, that you're not going to be in his pockets)-but *if he's not ready for a serious relationship,*

he going to treat you like sports fish."

— Steve Harvey

Chapter 13

Barbara

Barbara was divorced about 3 years ago. Her ex-husband was five years her junior and left her for much younger woman. I was 10 years older than Barb, a strict vegetarian -- "I don't like to eat anything that has blood in it." The way she said that, I understood her point even though I enjoy a great steak. She was a strict vegan and her right man *had* to be a vegan -- she didn't want to cook two meals each night. If she could meet a vegan and get a spark, then that's all she seemed to want.

She had a dog, lived alone, worked in an office and enjoyed cycling for hours and hours. She had a simple life but you could easily tell from her lonely eyes she was adrift in the world searching for someone to love again.

After meeting her and discussing our backgrounds, I asked her, "Since your divorce, have you had any relationships?"

"Just a few. Haven't really met anyone I like. I probably won't like you either! Haha! Seriously, before I got your message, I was going to quit looking and not force myself to meet anyone, but you looked okay and thought it would be nice to meet you.

"Sounds, like you really want to meet someone offline? You just want it to happen?"

"I really don't care if I meet anyone or not." She said.

I don't know why, but I didn't believe her, so I continued. "But, it's hard to meet anyone offline. If you see someone you'd like to meet on the street, or in a bar, or wherever, it's difficult since you don't know if they're married, etc. I enjoy meeting women online since it saves a lot of time finding available women."

"I think it's awkward. Like it's your turn on the stage and you've got to act your best." She said.

How true, I thought. "I know what you mean." "At first there's an awkward feeling to meet someone you've haven't ever seen before, but after a few meetups with different new people, you become more relaxed. Most of the people you meet feel just as awkward as you."

We talked on and on.

I liked her. I don't know why. She was younger but had a maturity and an uncomplicated life which attracted me. She wasn't a demanding person or aggressive, and I simply thought it would be nice to get to know her better. So, I simply said, "Hey, I feel I'm probably too old for you, especially since you were married to a younger man, but I'm not doing anything tonight. Let's go out."

She didn't reply. I could tell she wasn't interested in me since I wasn't a vegan and probably too old for her, but I continued, "Hey, if it doesn't work out, we can at least get to know each other? I can tell you about my online dating experiences and it might help you meet your perfect man -- if there is such a thing?

"Haha." She laughed.

I picked her up that evening and took her to a casual restaurant. I knew we weren't going further since I wasn't about to become a vegan even though it seemed healthy.

"So, let's say you join a vegan club and you meet someone. You said before you've got to get a spark when you see him. Tell me about the 'spark'. I'm just curious about it."

"Oh, I don't know." Barb said.

"It's *interesting* to me. I'd like to know *why* women choose men. I'm just an average guy and I've got no idea on what women call a "Spark" – I guess you're talking about "Chemistry" between two persons?"

"Oh, well.... You're going to think I'm from outer space, but when I meet a man whom I'm attracted to, I get a blue spark – like a miniature blue lightning bolt in the middle of my chest that flashes downward."

"You kidding?"

"No, it's real."

"Blue?"

"Yes, it's blue. I felt a spark and the color blue when I first met my husband and I get it when I see a good looking man on the street.

Other girls I know get the same blue spark."

    Amazing, I thought. This woman is telling me her secret truth. But what the hell? *Blue?*

"Barb, how do you feel the color blue?"

    "Okay, when I see an attractive man, my body feels a blue spark which starts in the area of my navel. It's like a bolt, a flash of white blue lightning in my body and my brain, and it goes downward...."

I was now on the edge of my seat looking at her stomach area. *Yeah, down ward is good,* I thought. Then shook my head and sat back.

"Thanks Barb, that's amazing!" We talked on and I gave her my version of how I react when I see a woman who is attractive to me. No blue spark but a surge of warmth, excitement, then kind of an alert-relaxed state comes over me.

We had a good time but the both of us knew it wouldn't work since I wasn't ready to become a vegan. We are still friends today.

Bruce Miller

"If a man loves a woman's soul, he'll end up loving one woman, but if he loves a woman's face, all the women in the world won't satisfy him."

-- Anonymous

Chapter 14

Gloria

I came across a woman online by accident – I was searching locally but inadvertently put in the wrong search area and came up with a gallery women living 100 miles away from me. I was about to close the page when Gloria's picture caught my eye. Her profile said she loved golf (I do too). We messaged back and forth, talked golf, golf courses and golf clubs on the phone and arranged to meet at a café near her, have lunch, then go for a walk where she would show me her town.

As I walked into the café, she was sitting at front table excited, smiling and happily waving at me. I felt awkwardly over-welcomed for someone she hadn't met before. Maybe single golfer guys are difficult to find -- I didn't know?

"Thanks for driving out. It's great to meet you!" She said.

Bruce Miller

"The long drive isn't bad when you have such a nice welcoming smile. I'm happy to meet you too!" I connected with the energy she had. Distance isn't a factor when you meet someone you really like. What a great first impression! I was excited to learn more about her.

We ordered lunch and the talk was continuous. She was easy to look at and I was feeling very positive about her.

"So tell me again about your Needle Pines Golf Club?" She asked. I told her about the club and her eyes widened as I talked about it. She continued, "My ex and I use to golf with Frank Bernat and his wife. They moved to your area some time ago. Do you know Frank Bernat?"

"Yes, I do. He's a great golfer and I've played with him several times. He and his wife used my vacation home for a week last year. They're great people. Wow, what a coincidence you know him." I said.

"How is Frank doing?"

"Well I guess life is great for Frank. He's always even tempered – just a normal guy. His wife plays with the regular ladies group on Tuesdays and Thursdays, but she's got about a 32 handicap and just plays to socialize. Frank's a single digit." I said.

"Yes, he is quite a man. We always had a great time with them."

We finished lunch and went for a walk. We talked about swimming, golf, her family, my family. After walking around town for an hour, she walked me over to her home. We went in and sat down. Since Frank was a mutual friend, our conversation turned to him.

"When you see Frank again, will you say 'Hi' to him for me?"

"Of course. I run into him now and then in the restaurant at the club and will say hello for you."

She stopped talking for a moment, then looked up at me and said, "I want to tell you something about Frank, but you have to promise me not to repeat it to him or to anyone?"

"Okay." I said. This was odd?

"Remember, you can't repeat this."

"Yes, okay?"

"I'm going to tell you a story about Frank and when I finish you'll know why you can't repeat it." She paused and stared at me, then said, "Do I have your solemn promise not to repeat this?"

"Yes, fine."

"When I was going through my divorce, I was alone a lot. We didn't have kids and it was difficult for me – my husband left to marry his personal assistant."

"Oh, sorry to hear that."

"Yeah, but I'm over it. I was around Frank and his wife at our golf club and Frank was very sympathetic toward me. He told me he was thinking of divorcing Doreen. He had lost any interest in having sex with her. She was overweight, not very healthy, and he told me they hadn't had sex in 5 years."

"Whoa, I can see why you don't want this repeated. This *really* isn't any of my business?" I wasn't sure I wanted to hear the rest, but she kept talking.

"Frank told me he wanted to have sex with me. He said since he hadn't had sex in such a long time, he was going to 'devour me.'"

"Yeah, I think I understand? Devour sounds good?" I joked trying to lighten the conversation.

"Oh yeah, 'Devour' sounded very good! But we didn't."

"Well, I admire your self-control. You were in the dumps over your divorce and Frank is a good looking man, so I'm sure that wasn't easy." I said.

"Hey, we should have lunch together at your club. I would love to see Frank again. I haven't seen him since he and Doreen moved away."

The picture came into focus. She knew I was from the suburb where Frank and Doreen were living. I figured her over excitement in meeting me was connected to seeing Frank again. She read my face.

"I don't ever want to come between Frank and Doreen. I just want to see them again and say hello."

Yeah right. But, then again, I might be thinking too much over nothing? Frank and Doreen seemed like a happy couple to me? Gloria was attractive and Frank must've had a weak moment? But it wasn't any of my business to know this, and Gloria comes out with this story at our first meet? Ah, too complicated.

"Yeah, sure, Gloria, that would be nice to have you come up for round. I could invite Frank and Doreen to play with us?" I added.

She was wringing her hands now. "Oh my, what am I doing? I don't want to have lunch at your club. I couldn't help myself. I think about Frank. Nope, I won't be up for lunch, at least not yet." She was confused and I felt sorry for her.

Our conversation dwindled. I politely told her as I left we should get together again. But this was all too complicated for me. I think she knew that already. As I drove back I reflected of her plan to use me to get to Frank. I didn't know it then, but I was going to meet a truly

Bruce Miller

two-faced woman, and I mean that literally, in the next chapter.

"My grandmother always used to wear this English perfume called Tuberose and then she died and then I dated this girl who wore the same thing. Every time I hung out with her, I could only think of my recently deceased grandmother. So sometimes a signature scent can be good and sometimes it can be bad."

-Mark Ronson

Bruce Miller

Chapter 15

Hilda

The 166th episode of the sitcom, "Seinfeld" was about Jerry meeting a "two faced" girl who looked extremely attractive, yet at other times, looked extremely ugly depending upon lighting or shadowing. Everyone seems to have a double appearance depending on lighting. Sometimes, I see myself looking so bad in pictures, I can't even recognize myself.

When Hilda walked into the dark café for our first meet, I shuddered at the way she looked. Unkempt, extremely thin, a strange odor from strong perfume (like formaldehyde) etc. I'm smart enough to know that a person's "looks" are secondary. There's a lot of men in the world, and if she took the time to meet me, then I will definitely respect that, subject, of course, to the "Picture Rule" of online dating: *"If you don't look anything like the person in your online picture, you're buying me drinks 'till you do."*

The conversation went slow at first, then we continued talking very naturally. We seemed to be on the same wave length and talked for two hours without realizing the time. She had her own business, was highly intelligent, kind, and very understanding. I was hooked and asked her out right away. She didn't dress well, her hair was average, and had a raspy voice. As we were leaving, sunlight caught her face just outside the door and she was instantly gorgeous. Her hair sparkled in the sun. My mouth fell open! I didn't say a word but I knew she could easily tell I was hooked.

   I picked her up for dinner at her home in a nearby suburb. She walked out the door in a tight fitting black skirt highlighting her trim waist and wide hips. She read me well seeing how amazed I was at her looks. She told me more about herself as we drove to the restaurant about 20 minutes away. We were going out on a date like teenagers and we talked about her high school cheerleading days, and teenage fun. The conversation turned to sex. She freely talked about it and I was getting too much information when she told me she lost her virginity in high school.

Not wanting to appear like a prude, I went with it and asked, "How'd that happen?" She described it in detail.

I got an erection listening to her and thought about making a U Turn and go back to her house. Then I'd glance at her face in the dark car and she was instantly ugly in the shadows. She made me horny, and she was a quality woman, so I didn't care. I thought I had found the "One". Then I got a stifling headache from her perfume.

"What perfume do you use?" I asked.

"Oh, do you like it?"

"I'm not sure, what's it called?" She gave me a French name.

"It's my favorite." She said.

"I'm not certain of this but I think I may have an allergy to something in it?"

"Oh?"

Bruce Miller

"Next time we pass the right store, you and I are going to select a perfume that you and I like together. We'll call it 'Kiss Me.'" I said.

She laughed.

She didn't wear the perfume again. We continued seeing each other but Hilda seemed to lose interest in me and I don't know why. I might have been too prudish, too much a gentleman, or just simply dull. I wasn't really keen on Hilda either, and I didn't fall head over heels over her, but I did with the woman in the next chapter.

"You can never control who you fall in love with, even when you're in the most sad, confused time of your life. You don't fall in love with people because they're fun. It just happens."

-Kirsten Dunst

Chapter 16

Cathy

My first impression of Cathy was she seemed to have a permanent smile embedded on her face in a very relaxed and happy way. She wasn't in gaga land. Rather, she had a beautiful and pleasant smile that was always there emanating from her soul. I was attracted to her instantly.

After giving our brief histories, I learned she had been widowed after a being married to a wonderful man. His death was sudden and unexpected and she missed him very much although two years had passed.

She told me about the wonderful life she had. A beautiful home, a cottage on the lake, a nice boat, regular vacations, lots of the good things in life. A very tough act to follow, I thought. She was, of course, still in love with him and just decided to try the dating site since she like anyone else gets lonely. I was her first date. We talked for two hours about her life. I wasn't sure if she liked me or was just very lonely.

"Sounds like you and John enjoyed life to the fullest. I'm no slouch, but sounds like he's irreplaceable."

"No one's ever going to take the place of John. But since he died, I don't get social invitations we use to get when he was alive. Say, you want to go up to my cottage on the lake? I'm usually there alone and the company would be nice."

"Sure." I answered. She was moving very fast, I thought, but that was fine with me and made me wonder why she didn't want to shop around awhile.

Well, she fit me into her life quickly. As far as I could tell, I wasn't ever going to replace John or even come close to it. I liked her very much. She was great looking, had a happy disposition and the invitations began again as she told everyone we were a couple.

I found myself falling for her. Yet, when I tried to express my growing feelings towards her, she would instantly back pedal leaving me with the impression she wasn't ready to live with anyone. I continued to wear my strong feelings for her on my sleeve (I couldn't help it). Every time I'd give her my best genuine and heartfelt romantic look, she'd return a happy, but neutral smile.

Her impartial smile devastated me. I was her handbag since at our first meet I must have met all her handbag criteria and she didn't need to shop further. She was still in love with her husband.

Stupidly, I accepted being taken off the shelf when needed and put back on the shelf when she was done with my stupid wishful thinking she'd become fonder or accustomed to me. As I looked to the future, I was in a quandary picturing myself being totally used by a woman, but used for a life of parties, mingling with happy people. Then I thought, how lucky is that?

I realized I would have a fun life with Cathy except, I had to live alone on the nights we weren't together and I'd have to give up my search for the soul mate I was trying to perhaps

foolishly find? I was being used in a very nice

way that most men would envy. I came to

realize I wouldn't ever totally win her heart

which her magnificent husband had locked up.

So I left Cathy, depressed and wondering if I

would ever find anyone to love, until I met the

girl in the next chapter.

I Came I Saw I Coffeed

"Well, Rhonda you caught my eye,

And I can give you lotsa reasons why

You gotta help me Rhonda

Help me get her out of my heart."

- The Beach Boys

Chapter 17

Denise

Sitting by myself in the clubhouse after a round of early morning golf, I pondered whether I should've given Cathy more time than the 4 months we'd been together. My thoughts were interrupted by approaching footsteps and a sweet voice, "Heard you broke up with

Cathy?" Raising my head, I saw Denise who I didn't know very well standing there smiling at me.

"Hi Denise. How are you?" Denise sat down at the table and made herself at home. I didn't know very much about Denise. An average looking woman and a widow like Cathy. Her husband, a successful land developer, had a sudden heart attack in his prime.

"You look glum? Tell me about it."

Bruce Miller

I simply said it didn't work out (not wanting be accused of feeling sorry for myself).

"Well there are plenty of other fish in the sea." Denise continued. "And there's not very many fishermen, eh…single men around?" I began to smile.

"Thanks Denise. You are – "

"Have you had lunch yet?" She interrupted.

"No."

"Come over to my place and I'll make you lunch."

Oh, I don't want to bother you." I said, feeling very stupid and depressed about leaving Cathy.

"No trouble? C'mon...." Denise lived nearby and sat me down at the kitchen table while she began making lunch. Light romantic music was emanating from the sound system while she worked on lunch in perpetual motion. She pushed open the glass patio doors leading out to the sea. The sea breeze tousled her hair over one dark brown eye and she seemed to brushed it back in slow motion. I was transfixed.

"Why don't you go downstairs and get a bottle of wine from the cellar?"

My trance was broken. "Okay! What are we having?"

"I'm not sure yet. Ah, get a red or whatever you want. Anything's fine with me." I spent a few minutes in the wine cellar then came up the stairs with a bottle hearing the oven door close.

"How is this?" I showed her the wine.

"Oh I got that in Italy." She went on telling me about Italy and sat down on the stool next to me with her face about 7 inches from mine. I was about to give her a friendly kiss on the cheek when the oven dinged. She jumped off the stool, handed me two plates, and told me to set the table and open the wine. She continued her perpetual motion lunch making still talking about Italy. She carried two dishes with something circular and steaming on each of them with thin spiraling bread sticks coming out the top. No tuna fish sandwich today, I thought.

"Wow! What are we having!" I said.

"Oh, just something I whipped up."

"Smells fantastic!"

We talked about her cooking and the more I praised it, the more she fussed about how it was nothing. We talked for an hour and discussed going out together. And, I was told in no uncertain terms if we casually dated, it had to be exclusive? We didn't discuss sex. I could well understand if you're having sex you should of course be exclusive. But she wanted instant steady dating. If we didn't get along, I was then free to date whoever I wanted (except for a woman she didn't like at the golf club – I didn't like her either) but absolutely no dates while I was dating her. I didn't mind following her orders.

My thoughts of Cathy disappeared and a new adventure was starting. Neither of us knew where it would lead. I agreed to begin instant steady dating.

Bruce Miller

We both enjoyed a few dates, but sad to say no chemistry developed. I wasn't disappointed when we agreed to go our own ways. She got me back on my feet. When I left Cathy, my thoughts went back to starting again on the dating site and reflected back to the first woman I met on line.

"Ladies let me give you some advice. You can throw all your ... chick-lit, self-help, why-doesn't-he-love-me books out, because this is all you need to know: Men will treat you the way you let them. There is no such thing as "deserving" respect; you get what you demand from people... if you demand respect, he will either respect you or he won't associate with you. It really is that simple." — Tucker Max, *I Hope They Serve Beer in Hell*

Chapter 18

Stella

The very first woman I met online after my unwanted divorce was Stella -- a very attractive brunette who sold real estate and agreed to meet after she got off work at a seaside lounge she picked for a glass of wine. I arrived 10 minutes early and watched Stella walking slowly on the beach approaching the restaurant. She was dressed in white shorts and a black tank top which showed off her great figure. Being recently divorced and nervous, I felt good since I was doing something to improve myself. I also got the impression she had performed her slow approaching beach walk to this meeting place before, but didn't mind since she looked great.

      Stella had only been on line for a while looking for a partner. She laughed when I told her she was the very first lady I arranged to

Bruce Miller

meet. She had met several men on line but didn't give me any details about them which I liked. I didn't want to hear about the competition just yet.

We gave each other our backgrounds, then talked casually. I focused on her eyes when she talked so it was easier to get to know her personality – something hard to do when messaging back and forth on a dating site.

We finished our wines and decided to walk the beach. Being brand new at this, I didn't want to appear forward so I didn't try to hold her hand as we walked -- just let my arms swing. I started to relax then tried to hold her hand to show her I was interested. She pushed my hand away and pressed my upper right arm against the side of her breast. I smiled feeling like we were old friends rather than someone I'd met 30 minutes ago.

Then her phone rang.

She looked at her phone and dismissed the incoming call and smiled at me. My smile got bigger.

"Hey, Stella, please take any calls. I understand real estate agents work 24/7!"

"Sorry, that wasn't a business call."

"Well, you *are* a very attractive lady and I'm sure you've got a lot of men calling you."

She paused and looked at me and said, "Wish I had the good ones calling me." I was smiling big time now.

Her phone made a tone. A text came in.

"Hey, someone's persistent." I said. Stella pulled out her phone. Looked at it and shot a short message back.

"If you have to be somewhere, that's fine. I'd like to see you again." I asked.

"Yes, I'd like to see you again too." Her phone gave off another tone. She looked at it and shook her head.

"You having trouble with someone?" I asked.

"No, a friend of my stepson's is asking if I want chicken tonight."

I was puzzled. During our wines, Stella told me she had a 20-year-old stepson learning the construction trade. She saw my look.

"He lives with me. There's nothing romantic going on."

That was a little more than I wanted to hear. My curiosity grew. "Has he lived with you long?"

"About a year."

"How old is he?"

"Oh around 40."

Yeah right, I thought, "Nothing romantic going on" really means nothing romantic going on right now, or anymore, or what? She read my face again.

"I've been trying to get him out of my place."

"Sounds complicated." I said.

"Yeah, he sometimes follows me and I've got to get him out of my life."

"Why don't you just ask him to leave?"

"He won't."

"Well, seems you've got a few options, you could see a lawyer, get him evicted..."

"No I wouldn't do that."

"Is he working?"

"No. Hey, I know this sounds very strange but he told me he killed a man in self-defense. He's very well mannered, always a gentleman, but I'm afraid of him." This was too much information. She read my face and started walking away from me.

"Are you in any danger from him?"

"He stalks me."

I looked around and felt sorry for her. "I have a friend who is a police sergeant who told me a lot of this goes on all the time. The police are familiar with these situations and all you have to do is to visit a police station and they will help you."

"No. He might do something to me."

She began to walk away again. But I had to try and help, "Can I walk you anywhere?"

"No thanks. That's nice you're concerned. Here's my card if you want to get together again."

I took her card and smiled but didn't say anything as she left.

A year later, I ran into her again on the street. Her stalker roommate had moved; she was living alone and still looking for a partner. We are still friends today. After meeting Stella,

I Came I Saw I Coffeed

I got a good dose of meeting the wrong woman in the next chapter.

"I was asked what I was looking for in a relationship. Apparently "A way out" wasn't the right answer."

-Rebel Circus

Chapter 19

Brenda

Brenda's profile showed we were the same age. Her pictures looked fine and we had similar backgrounds. When she walked into the café, I didn't recognize her. Her hair was a different color. She looked tired with her eyes half open. It was 9:00am in the morning. She walked toward me like she was on the last mile of a twenty-mile uphill hike. I scrambled to my feet after realizing it was her. She gave me a long hug. She hadn't washed.

"Hi Brenda, very nice to meet you." I said.

"Yes, nice to meet you too, Bob."

"Ah, my name is Bruce." I smiled.

"Oh sorry."

I ordered coffee for us and looked at her. She was staring at me like Vanessa's dog, Max, but meaner. Her arms were crossed. She was much older than her pictures.

Since she bothered to take the time to meet me, I smiled and asked, "How long have you been on the dating site?"

She paused, then inhaled mucus inside her nose before speaking. "I don't know. It's been a while."

I looked for the door feeling cheated. Perhaps she's not honest or maybe just lazy about updating her picture? I didn't want to figure it out. But, maybe there's more to her? I smiled and tried to see if I could get a smile from her. "Tell me about yourself?"

She looked away. Her phone beeped and she pulled it out and returned a message. While she was texting, I looked her over and figured she must have slept late – just gotten out of bed?

She finished texting, then looked at me and looked away again. As she was looking at the wall, she told me about herself. No eye contact, no smile, I decided 15 minutes would be enough.

    We casually talked and she relaxed a bit but still no smile. I don't usually make people nervous but she was nervous about something. Does she really want to meet someone? Maybe I was too young for her? Why didn't she change her way too young picture to what she really looks like? I could only guess. I didn't want to know her story. Maybe she took one look at me and decided this wasn't going to work? The small talk continued. We finished our coffee, I

Bruce Miller

thanked her for coming and walked her to the

door. Then I met an exceptional woman.

"It's not you, it's me. I'm just totally not interested in you."

-Anonymous

Bruce Miller

Chapter 20

Roberta

Roberta had a brief and an average to above average profile. I later learned when I met her in person she was actually a high powered business woman who ran her own Public Relations firm.

I Came I Saw I Coffeed

I sat in the café looking forward to our meet reading her profile on my iPad and reading it again (between the lines) I got a second impressions she was very active and full of life. She was recently divorced and only had one headshot of herself on the site. I liked her average look.

I was still reading her profile when I heard the sound of high heels clicking toward me and looked up. Roberta ("Bobbie") looked amazing! White blouse with a black skirt and black high heels with a multi-colored silk scarf around her neck. She wore quiet, tasteful jewelry and revealed an expensive watch as she planted her designer handbag on the table. She greeted me with a smile followed by a warm a kiss on the cheek. I had met many women from the dating site, but Bobbie, by far, was one of the happiest, most self-assured woman I had met. For some unknown reason, she put an unflattering picture of herself of the dating site.

"It's very nice to meet you, Bruce." As we ordered coffee and I thanked God I asked to meet this woman. We talked about her life, her work, her past relationships, etc. As she talked her shoulder length silken brown hair flowed down to her shoulders shimmering as she spoke. This mesmerizing lady super salesperson brought back a memory about a brief court hearing I attended where the opposing lawyer was super attractive woman resembling Bobbie. When the lady lawyer made her argument at podium in front of the judge, all eyes were on her. When it was my lawyer's turn to present our position, she flipped her hair and locked eyes with the judge while my lawyer was arguing our case. We lost that court hearing and wished we had a woman judge.

Bruce Miller

Bobbie impressed me a great deal and I asked her out for a dinner on the weekend, but she had plans. I asked about the next weekend but she was non-committal so I just marked her up as one of the girls my grandmother told me about.

Bruce Miller

"Women draws her life from man, and gives it back again. And there is love…."

-Noel (Paul) Stookey

Chapter 21

Janet

When I met Janet I didn't feel amazed, and no fireworks were going off in my head. There wasn't any strong chemistry either. I was getting tired of meetups. Janet had just got on line after being widowed three years ago. There wasn't anything special about her. She dressed normally, nothing flashy, had average looks and I didn't expect it to go any further.

She asked me about myself and I gave her my history and then I asked about her. She didn't say anything exciting or unusual, just related her average life to me which was abruptly broken by the sudden death (heart attack) of her husband. Her friends helped her though it. She just got on line out of curiosity.

She liked golf, and keeping fit (as I did as well), but we talked on and on and without realizing it, two hours had passed. She seemed to well understand most everything I said and likewise I understood her feelings when she talked. We dated. I really didn't know if I would fall in love with her but I did. She understood my nature and I understood her. It was a naturally growing attraction. Nothing special either of us did, her replies and my replies in conversations seemed like puzzle pieces effortlessly fitting together. She enjoys living with me and vice versa. Maybe this is what people mean when they talk about falling in love when you least expect it.

Our minds mated us. Not our looks, nor our likes or dislikes. Have you've ever had a best friend who sincerely listens...and I believe that's what first made me very attracted to her. She listened to my babble sincerely. She would respond telling me of similar events in her life which I listened to with interest.

There weren't any fireworks going off in my mind - just a growing appreciation toward her personality and as we understood each other more, she automatically became more

Bruce Miller

attractive to me even though she probably only had a casual average look. Nothing special at all.

    I sincerely felt the way she listened to me and the way I listened to her we could have both been fat, bald, mismatched heights, have bad manners, etc. etc. and it wouldn't have made any difference. She didn't look like my beloved mother or anyone I knew before. She was just – Janet.

    I wish I could give all women advice on how to have a man call you back. Deep down, I think it's simply of matter of being sincere and being yourself and to be calm about it. You don't have to show you're interested in his looks, or money, or physique, or position in life. You just sincerely show your interest in him by talking to him what your interests and asking about his interests. Usually the more you listen to him will make him feel more eased with you and if you can get him to be relaxed, that's all the better since people are at their best when they are relaxed usually.

 I used to be flattered when a woman would say I was the most brilliant lawyer on earth, but I knew that wasn't true. It raises my ego for a few seconds, but the rush of a nice compliment soon dissipates into feelings of hearing insincerities.

What made me interested in Janet and what made me want to call her back was she:

- Looked me steadily in the eyes when I spoke, and I found myself steadily looking into her eyes when she spoke.
- She didn't have to repeatedly text me or call me or approach me after

our first meet. If she did, I most likely would not have pursued her. I don't mind a woman following up and texting me as long as she is sincere about it and brief.

- She didn't flirt with me. She was nice looking and occasionally other men would approach her. She told me, "Men at times hit on me, but I have a look which I use which stops most of them." That made me feel she was a woman who knew what

Bruce Miller

she wanted and was mature about

life and the adventures life offers.

- When we started to live together,

we both don't want to get into

each other's faces during the day

and did our own thing and then

talked about our days in the

evening.

- She was very patient and at no

time did she ever force the

conversation. She just remained

quiet if she had nothing to say.

- Another thing that made me call her back was she was not judgmental and while she had opinions, I had to ask her what her views were as she wouldn't volunteer criticism on issues. When I asked her about how she felt about an issue, I would get a straightforward and sincere answer. She was a bit introverted which made her mysterious to me at first and as I learned more about

Bruce Miller

her likes and dislikes my attraction grew and grew.

- She didn't ever criticize herself either and that made me aware she was someone who demanded respect.

Anyway, I don't know if the above will give you any insight on why a man would call a woman back after the first meet. I just did since she intrigued me, and I was more intrigued as we talked and talked. She was just herself and I knew she was simply a sincere person who didn't play games.

I Came I Saw I Coffeed

It was a gradual growing attraction and relationship. In other words, my view is we shouldn't try to find or force love, or force or trick the man into calling you back. Try letting love find you. "Falling in love" actually means "falling" because you don't force yourself to fall, you just find yourself falling into it.

I hope this book is helpful to you and you enjoyed the stories.

Bruce Miller

Thank you for purchasing this book. I hope you found it useful and entertaining, and my views gave you some insight into the seemingly complex world of relationships.

If you enjoyed it, please consider leaving a review on Kobo or Goodreads or Amazon so more readers can find this title.

I sincerely wish you the best if you are seeking a partner.

I would like to hear from you if you have any questions or comments and you can contact me through our website TeamGolfwell.com. Thank you.

Kind regards,

Bruce Miller JD

Other books by Bruce Miller

Beware the Ides of March: A Novel Based on Psychic Readings

Dragonflies: A Novel Based on What Men Think of Women

Latecomers To Love: Online Dating for Mature Men and Women: Why Didn't He Call Me Back? Why Didn't She Want a Second Date? First Online Meetup Impressions from a Man and a Woman

www.ingramcontent.com/pod-product-compliance
Lightning Source LLC
Chambersburg PA
CBHW011406070526
44577CB00003B/388